A Climb Back Up
by Matthew Cipolla

"This is what you look like when you succeed!"
-Frank Cipolla
August 31, 1946-November 30, 2008

All rights reserved.

Published by Matthew Cipolla
through CreateSpace

Copyright © 2013

This book is protected under the copyright laws of the United States of America. Any reproduction or other unauthorized use of the material or artwork herein is prohibited without the express written consent of the author.

Back Cover/Inside Photographs: taken by Matthew Cipolla

Printed in the United States of America: March, 2013

ISBN-13:978-0615775104
ISBN-10:0615775101

For my dad and
the family that I love

"Another Beautiful Day."

A Therapeutic Means of Overcoming Pain

breathe in
hold tight
think

let your emotions
bleed –glorious black ink
staining the white
on the page.

Don't Hold in the Pain

let it be heard
let it be known

The way may seem lost
in the wake of a treacherous mountain
sprouting high, through the blackened clouds.

Climb back up – to freedom
through the rain and dismal dark
you will find your worth at the peak
where the sun burns bright

You owe it to yourself to Survive

Contents

C

My story 6

Part I

The Last Painting I Remember Before My Father Died 16

Come Back 17

First Steps 18

Velcro Sky 19

The Cheetah's Stride 21

Chill 23

The Living World 24

Who Killed the Man of Steel? 25

The Funeral Home 26

Lying Awake 27

Faith in E-flat Minor 28

Trapped 29

Alcohol 30

No God	31
In My Hands	32
Destruction	33
Northern Peace of Mind	34
Pictures on the Monitor	35
My Brother Came From Arizona When He Heard the News	36

Part II

The Sideline	38
A Climb Back Up	40
Normalcy	43
Poem to Myself	44
I Was Once Told	45
Life's a Stage	46
Science Experiment	47
Repelling	49
Near Death	50
The Best of the Worst Circumstance	51
Dreams Come True	52
Secret Family Recipe	53

The Expendables	54
Hard to Keep Up?	55
A Beautiful Day	56
Wilson's Mesa	57
Questions	58

Part III

With Nothing But a Shadow	62
An Open Letter	63
Snow Shoes and Raw Meat	64
Threads	65
Drowning Man	66
Lost at Sea	68
The Man in Chains	69
Empty Shell	70
Grab Hold (With Fear of Falling)	71
Nose Hairs	73
All Along	74
Colors	76
Between Two Stone Pillars	77

Running With Cheetahs	
	80
Scattered Stones	
	81
Reminiscing with Dragonflies	
	82
Upon the Shell of a Turtle	
	83
One White, One Black	
	84
Balloon	
	86
The Necklace (A Climb Back Up Part 2)	
	87

My Story:

The phone call came as my brother Andy and I were heading home down I-275 towards Toledo, with cries from our mother telling us to return home as quickly and as safely as possible. She told us how dad was being taken to the hospital in an ambulance.

We were both shocked, but ignorant to the fact of what could have been. *This was the man that could never die.* My dad was active and fit. He ran almost every day and was as healthy as can be. But this just goes to show, nobody is safe; death comes when it's least expected.

My brother and I joked about the potential causes of what could possibly land him in the hospital, but that's all it was, a joke.

As the car sped down the highway we made our way back home. Andy, must have been distracted by something because we missed our exit, but before long we made it home.

We returned home to an empty house and a ringing phone; our uncle Frank telling us to get to the hospital. It was here that Andy knew something was wrong. I, on the other hand, was clueless to this fact.

"Be prepared," my brother kept telling me. The words sunk in, but only for a moment. I didn't give them a chance. I didn't need to be prepared. We were going to show up at the hospital and discover that everything was perfectly fine. At that moment death was the furthest thing from my mind.

I'd be a liar if I said it didn't cross my mind once or twice, but this was the man that could never die, so it was crazy to think that was even a possibility.

He was having the best day of his life prior to this. We left church that Sunday morning. And right on cue, as he always did, the man called out, "Another Beautiful Day," and it was. It *always* was.

The pampering white of the snow flung across the ground. It was a glorious winter morning.

With the snow covered ground and a full wallet the man was ready for the day. We went out to breakfast that morning, like we did every Sunday morning when we were kids. It was always a great time: Two eggs over medium, white toast, a side of sausage, and a nice cold chocolate milk.

Mom and dad stirred in their cream and sugar, bringing the hot coffee to their lips with a loving connection. I wish Andy could have been their to enjoy this moment, to see how happy he was.

I could only imagine what was going through the man's mind. I wonder; did he know he was going to die? Did he expect that his heart might give way? Knowing him, even if he felt it, I bet he ignored the signs. That's how he was. He was the man that could never die and I'll be damned if he didn't think that himself. He looked out into the world. The snow fell from the sky, and he saw opportunity. The perfect day to run; nothing was going to stop him from slipping on those shoes and enjoying the day.

That day, my brother and I went to the Detroit Institute of Art, something I needed to do for school. Curiosity often hits me when I remember this little detail, because my dad was going to go with me if Andy didn't. What if he hadn't? What if my dad had gone with me instead? Would things have played out differently? Would he still have died? I often wonder.

As we got into the car for the second time, following the calls from uncle Frank, we made our way to the hospital. I could tell Andy was getting more and more worried as his grip tightened around the steering wheel. His shoulders tensed and his eyes remained fixed, concentrated on the road. I wanted to tell him that everything would be fine. But I couldn't say that, could I? What if I was wrong? But I didn't believe I was wrong, did I? The mind assumes the worst, I guess mine didn't get the memo.

We arrived to the hospital, through the entrance and down the hall; IDs pinned to our chests. The white hallway burned my eyes. It felt heavenly. It felt peaceful; like nothing was wrong. Looking back now, the heavenly sight must have been a sign of things to come; a sign of something that had to happen, whether we wanted it to or not; that wasn't up to us.

As we walked down the hallway Andy's words continued to pulse through my mind, "Be prepared." I shook them off once more. There was nothing that could have prepared me, not even if the hallways were stained red, would I have believed the words that came next.

We arrived at the waiting room where we were met by three familiar faces, a look of sully stained in their eyes. I felt the blatant stares of my father's two best friends as I sat on the couch and Andy followed suit beside me. I waited for answers, but was met with only silence. The silence remained until it was broken by Andy who spoke, "What's the word," he asked. His choice of words fumbled through my mind. I didn't understand them. I could hear the gulp in his tone. It felt as if he didn't know what to say, as if he just needed to break the silence. And when he did; he wished he hadn't.

The two friends gazed over to Mike, my older brother, who sat in a chair at the opposite end of the room. I was eager to know that nothing was wrong. He looked up in disbelief. My eagerness faded. I could see the pale complexion on his face. And the second he spoke, I could tell, he had come to the realization, "Dad's dead."

What happened next I couldn't control. I fell inside my mind and shut out the world. I felt my face burn red and tears sizzle on my cheeks. Next thing I knew I was in the hallway staring at my devastated mother.

My heart stopped a few times as she cried, "They couldn't save my man." I felt the squeeze of togetherness. The familiar love of family trying to pull together as one. It was like a shock to the chest; a defibrillator sting and a voice inside screaming, *STAY WITH ME.*

We couldn't do this alone; with interlocking arms we walked towards the room. Slowly we shuffled, feet sliding across the bright white floor. Up ahead a doctor stood, clipboard in hand, he looked at me for a split second, I could see the disappointment in his eyes as he quickly looked away and glanced down at his clipboard, perhaps ashamed to look any longer, wishing he could turn back time, and try again, so he wouldn't have to see that look in my eyes.

I felt embarrassed, empty, and distraught. My heart was pounding rhythmically. It hurt to breathe, it hurt to see. And when I saw him, my eyes went blank. I turned away in an instant, holding the nearest person: mother, brother, aunt, cousin, I'm not sure who. I rubbed at my eyes tossing my glasses to the floor. I remember hearing the clang against the ground, as I thought, *I hope they broke.* I didn't want to see.

Next thing I know I'm in a chair, my head between my knees; hands gripping my hair, trying to wake myself up from this nightmare. How quickly things change from sunshine to rain; from a beautiful day to this. *Wake up, wake up. Please. Just wake up.*

More and more familiar faces shuffled in. My aunt (my father's sister) screaming, "Why, why, please God why?" My eyes remained fixed upon the floor. The tiles were dirty and I wanted to leave and tell someone to clean them; anything to get out of that room. But I stayed. I couldn't move. I was frozen in place, my body numb and my cheeks burning. After some time my glasses were returned to me and I finally found the courage to look up. My mother stood with my aunt. My aunt held his hand as she spoke, "He's so cold." My mother responded with, "You're never cold."

    I shook uncontrollably as I stood up and wandered into the hall. Up and down the hallway I walked, pacing back and forth running my hands along the wall. I walked back to the waiting room where my nephew laughed and played. There were people trying to explain to him what happened. He didn't understand. He just thought everyone was crazy for saying such a thing. *You and me both.*

    I continued to pace the hallway. I walked far, so far that I wondered if I was aloud to be where I was, but truthfully, I didn't care. I wanted to get as far away from this place as I could.

    My memory is hazy. There isn't much I can remember from this point on. There wasn't a *have a nice day* as we walked out the door. The car that pulled up, I couldn't tell you what it was. I couldn't tell you who was driving or who I sat next to; everything is a blur.

14

I remember our house didn't sound the same; everyone was speechless. It no longer had the feeling of home as I wandered through the haunting silence; walking around like I did at the hospital. I stayed in my mind and drowned everything else out; up the stairs and down the stairs.

A moment that I will never forget happened soon after. I stood at the far end of the room, frozen. I listened as my niece was told the news. My heart sank as she responded and kept repeating over and over, "But, I want him." She didn't understand that he wasn't coming home, "I want to see him."

I walked up stairs once more and stood in the doorway of my room. I stood there; staring at nothing. My mind was a mess, littered with emptiness. My heart fell flat as I thought, *How are we ever going to come back from this.*

Part I

Mt. Phillips. Cimarron, New Mexico. Elevation: 11,742 ft

The Last Painting I Remember Before My Father Died

The sandals stood in the sand, person-less and alone,
the tide flowing, removing any sign of footprints.

The wearer is long gone; left without a trace. He
told no one of his adventure; leaving all to wonder.

Where has this man gone? The only one who knows
the truth of the journeyed man remains upon the beach;

speechless, underneath the sea gull cries, the sandals
awaiting surrender, left behind in a clump. The sun

breaching the watered horizon, casts a shadow of light,
questioning the pair; it's effervescence shattered and

distraught for even he is unaware of where
the man has gone.

Come Back

i fail to see the beauty in this day, relish
emasculated in an instant. i pray we

make it through this; waiting on bended
knee for someone to roll the clock hillside,

and while my mind tumbles with
the minute hand, whirling rampant,

i think to myself, what life offers
is tactful catastrophe inflicted

with spurts of tasteless comfort. taste
burns and dwindles; creeping down

the back of my throat. i'm losing feeling
as i pick up speed. all i can see

are the daggered stones quickly
approaching at the bottom of the hill.

First Steps

Though I feel—buried in my tears,
up the path I begin the journey
through the abysmal disaster.

My hands breach the faceless
cave and I feel lost. My bare
feet shift through the dirt.

I am met with only darkness and
echoes indistinguishable nonsense.

My closed eyes guide the way as
my ears hinder my judgment.

Velcro Sky

I can feel your heart still beating,
the constant pitter patter against my chest.

Locked in tow
and shackled,

breathing as the walls close in
around me.

The tears chill my red hot flesh,
sizzle and then dissipate,

a mist,
then freedom.

Tear down these walls!
Release the bounds that coop

and cross me over into the relentless
night; to breathe in the curing air.

Without a cage I'd look
to the sky with velcro cries,

to lift and beat the law
that holds me down.

I'd break the chains
and float away

from every putrid cliche moment
and damned, I'm sorry

I wouldn't have to see
or hear or feel.

I'd be free to take my place. Hanging in
the sky—my face like the sun.

I'd shine righteous!
I'd shine forever

in the cold black night when all you can see
is the hand in front of your face

and you're clawing through the molten fog.
While you're lost, I'm right at home.

And while you're barred indoors
'cause the rain won't let you bloom.

I'll raise my soul to the highest peak
and break through the clouds and give

you something to look at. And you'll smile
and dream, to one day shine as bright as me.

The Cheetah's Stride

I feel like I'm running with the Cheetahs,
without a moment to stop and breathe.

I want to marvel at the wondrous
things this world has to offer,
but there's no time.

I want to remember my youth
my timeless imagination

I think, no
I need
I must
slow my stride

But suddenly
I feel the push,

the swift coursing wind,
my speed needs focus.

Within my own mind I fade,
trapped in a moment

when it's just me and a blank
savanna sheet looking back at me.

And I'm lost with the grass
towering above my head

the sun burning hot against
the nape of my neck. Sweat
pooling on the tip of my nose.

I fall to the dirt to be planted,

22

sprouting to release the pheromones
that draw time to a standstill,

as the Cheetahs
scatter around me.

Chill

After "Western Skyline" by Dawes

I get the feeling that he brought it here
and I never want it to go away

The snow fall crawling in the wind
like spiders swaying in the breeze

Stern gusts of wind flowing them over
rooftops with explosions against closed
window panes.

The Living World

It takes strength to live in the land of the living,
to ignore the constant utterances of the afterlife,

a heaven where your true love waits,
arms wide open, forever waiting

for your time to take hold of that
loving embrace.

That time isn't now,
you're not ready.

You're needed
here in a land
of purpose,

with the hearts that
look to you for help.

Motherhood lives on without
the father, we can't lose both.

"We do what we can to survive,"
that is what you told me.

But are we really
just trying to fit

in the living world? Making use
of this time we don't want?

What if I need it?
What if you need it?

Who Killed the Man of Steel?

I was 17 when Superman died of a heart attack.
All the bullets in the world couldn't penetrate his steel,
but I guess all that weight pulled heavy on his heart.

It happened on the first snow in November, as
his son, I wanted desperately to paint an "S"
on my chest, to be that same hero that flew

around the world. I'd turn back time and bring
back the sunrise. And with it, the stretching arms
and yawning cries; a blissfully calm Sunday

morning. The fluttering snow glistening through
the window, shimmering under the sun,
pampering the ground with a blanket.

And I'd search for the kryptonite that took
his life, and crush it beneath my feet

The Funeral Home

I tried to maintain a constant flow from head to toe
with a constant tremor lodged, trembling, at my core.

My weak knees harnessed only by whimsical puns
and *remember whens*. Piece by piece it reassembled

me, peace through peace we lied. Gathered in silence,
covering pain with flowers, familiar eyes all around

me. I could tell how lost everyone was, as we tried
to dislodge the boulder that covered the cave.

Lying Awake
After "Can't get it right today," by Joe Purdy

Days go by, weeks, months, years
and the pain is still there.

The pain will never go away. It will always lay
dormant, waiting for the inopportune moment
to explode.

Should I give up?

Faith in E-flat Minor
the song I played at the funeral

I approach the bench with angst
unaware of the melody that would make it's way
from fingertips pure.

The cling and scratch of nails on ivory keys.
A gentle touch, a caressing pull,
slide along the 52 albescent keys – a swelling of emotion, high
in the pit of my stomach, longing
for black.

I breathe and feel. Letting emotions seize control
of my soul

The anger burns in fiery eyes
twiddled fingers stuttering for answers
with a ferocious tremolo.

Let the octave singe—the piercing E flat.

The slam! A glissando enkindled with
a feeling of ease, longing for
the minor to fall.

A major need for recompense
slewed with denial eager to blindfold
my soul.

Flushing tears from cheek to ivory,
the dabbled drips breathing a melody
of sorrow.

With a drop of relinquish hope,
I am reborn. Ready to begin again.

Trapped

There's so much power in a word
so much therapy behind a gimmick
with aid gained from a scream

There is so much relief
to be had at the top of my lungs
and I intend to let it out.

Alcohol

I get why people do it; there is
such glorified indulgence
from ingested poison.

It kills
the pain.

And brings
life back.

But who are you when it takes over?
Just another statistic, floating in the breeze
becoming the definition of grievance.

Stepping back, farther
and farther; until
you are nothing,

but a washed up anchor
clawing at the shore.

No God

jumping gaps between
belief and disbelief.

    reason

        gone.

    hope

        gone.

In My Hands

I want to scream at the top of my
lungs to be heard, but I don't.

I keep my silence and watch
letting frustration seeps into

reality; my glossy eyes to cue
that this is real.

I reach out for a grasp of anything
pliable. In my grip, I bend to keep

myself sane, with deep breaths my
heart beat slows. My hands calm.

Destruction

The world was whole,
then nothing.

One harsh mess
of haunting silence, it

knows the love and learns
the noise. It breathes

for one, then all, then
all together nothing.

The world was empty,
searching for something.

Northern Peace of Mind

After "High Hopes," by Pink Floyd

The clouds breathe rain drops—
dwindling lightening claiming

the house for their own. I hold
my shoulders tight to keep warm,

as I walk outside, through open doors,
spinning in circles and tipping toes.

I watch as time roll in around
me. It surround and constrict

my being. I reach out into the distance
for some northern peace of mind;

spending a little more time
getting drenched to the bone.

Pictures on the Monitor

Alone I stare
my senses dwindle
as I lose my ears.

They fall to the floor
and gather in dust
unable to hear.

My hand grips the
mouse, rotating
hourglass.

Fingers like sand
crumbling beneath
my palm.

My lips sealed,
I cannot breathe
to scream.

But within my
chest, I feel a
pulsating beat.

My Brother Came From Arizona When He Heard the News

I stood on the third step as the door
slowly closed behind you.

The blankness on your face hurt me,
but your presence rearranged me.

I can't imagine what it was like to hear
from 2,000 miles away. The plane ride
over must have been hell.

You pull me in with a loving embrace
and I know—togetherness is what we
all need the most in this world.

Someone to squeeze the life out of you
because that, that is what brings you back.

Part II

Mt. Baldy. Cimarron, New Mexico. Elevation: 12,441.

The Sideline

You should have seen yourself,
in those short-shorts
swinging your hips
and patting your thighs

talk about embarrassing,

but, hell

I miss it.

Yes, there were those days when I
would lower my head and
say to myself, *I don't know
that guy. That's not my dad.
Oh my god! Are you fucking
kidding me!*

But that was just you. Being you.
That was how you lived. You
were just being

your crazy, ridiculous, center
of attention, *I don't care
what people think* self

What a way to live!

But behind that was something else.
something loving and caring.

You were always there, smiling,
cheering even when there was nothing to
cheer for,

at practice, while I was shooting hoops
or kicking the ball around in middle school.
And while I was running my heart out in high school.

It seemed unnecessary. And it annoyed me. Man
did it annoy me. But now that I think about it,
every game I ever played, every race I ever ran,
around every turn, I looked for your face
cheering wildly from the sideline.

And you always were.

But where are you now? Around every corner
I turn, every door I open, I look for you.

Where have you gone?

I always wonder.
But I can't shake the feeling
that you're here
next to me,

always,

on the sideline forever, cheering
me on, through every moment
of every day.

And that's a thought
worth living for.

A Climb Back Up

"This is what you look like when you succeed!"
- Frank Cipolla
August 31, 1946 – November
30, 2008

    An impossible climb to the
    highest peak.

    I look to the clouds knowing
    that I would soon be standing in heaven

    In a state of déjà vu, I remember the
    day we climbed this mountain together.

    I reached the top long before you.

    I waited
    and waited.

    Now, you're waiting
    for me.

    I take a step and begin my ascent.
    With a sip of water I feel at one with
    the world.

    I climb to you.

    Below,
    passersby dream
    of shaking hands with God—
    they live with patience.

    Teary eyes from a scorching sun,

I fall to my knees, weeping.
Breathless

With my head in the dirt
fingers scrapping the gravel
I hold onto your memory.

Breathe in,
Breathe out.

Breathe in,
Breathe out.

I force myself to my feet.
I rise then fall.

My weak knees too
brittle to continue.

I reach out,
        with clammy palms
        a broken soul,
I long to see you—one last time.

I feel the touch of peace, an angel, a touch
of strength,
of sweet serenity.
Grasping hands he pulls me to my feet,

with a hand on my shoulder, he guides me there,
ever closer to your side.

Through the tree line
into the arid sky.
I gasp for air as he sets me free,

to climb
alone

Piercing through the clouds, overcoming
weightlessness, into the moist atmosphere,
a breath of fresh air. I look to the
horizon, to the endless vision that is my world:

rolling hills,
open fields,
an abundance of green.

I sit alone on *your* bundle of rocks.
Uncomfortable
I adapt—within the shallow clouds—I wait.

Your voice hits me with a chilling calm,
"Another beautiful day."

Normalcy

I was lost and alone, friendless it seemed.
Untrue as that was I was unaware of how

to handle the change. I wanted to head
back to a normal life as soon as possible,

back to school—back to an imaginary world
of denial. I told myself to move passed it like

nothing had happened. In my disarray, I tried
to shut out the noise of a constantly sobbing

family. Their wide eyes left me feeling a loss
of belonging at times, because things never did

look the same and never would. Out in the world I
was treated differently, with unwanted sincerity, like

I was a stranger who's best chance of survival were
thumbs flipped up in approval and fake smiles telling

me to be happy; that I was okay. Moving on was a thing
of impossibility, but I kept my head down and took all

that I could get; no tests and special privileges. I don't
think that's what I needed, that wasn't the normalcy I

was searching for. But I took what I could get. For the
good of being *normal* and overcoming disaster. I wanted

to put on my shades, to play the role of the stranger, to
dabble in drugs and alcohol; to be a man that wasn't me.

Poem to Myself

i don't know how you do it,

happiness to sadness
in the blink of an eye.

the smile always returning.

I Was Once Told

I miss the good old days,
when a day was more than 24 hours,
it was an eternity.

Now the hours fly by and the years quickly follow.
They say time flies when your having fun,
well, I'm not having fun growing old.

I was once told, "Aging is mandatory,
but growing up is optional,"

so I'm gonna strap myself in and live my life,
but I'll never fully grow up.

I'm a poet, I'm a writer, an artist, a musician, the
pen decides my maturity. My instrument tells me
how to act.

Life's a Stage

The guitar sets the mood, as they cling to my stage.
I clear my throat and tap the beat on my knee.
This is me, breaking out of my cage.

I feel the beat, I breathe the words, and free the gauge
of worldwide cries, the beating hearts; a crowd that needs me.
The guitar sets the mood, as they cling to my stage.

Melody free me, hear me; let me feel the sweet disengage
from everything else but you. Guard lowered without plea;
this is me breaking out of my cage,

With the lock at the floor, I breathe life with a song.
It's a feeling of release, of safety, the way things should be.
The guitar sets the mood, as they cling to my stage,

Music can solve all our problems, if only for a moment.
We all need some hope. We need some melody, so let it be.
This is me, breaking out of my cage,

The world is a stage, and I'll sing, I'll play. I'll engage
in her, and her in me; within my palms to decree:
the guitar sets the mood, as they cling to my stage.

    This is me, breaking out of my cage.

Science Experiment

I held the cat in my hands, standing on top
of the stairs, playing the lion king.

I held her over the balcony
for all the animals to see

I look
I think
I ponder.

Cat—Balcony—Cat—Balcony
"Cats always land on their feet," I thought.

So I let her go,

down
down
down

she falls,
landing on her
feet.

I smile,

laughing, giggling, I run down
the stairs to scoop her up again.

"Cats, ALWAYS, land on their feet." I thought again.

So I dropped her again.

I laugh
I smile

48

And I scoop her up again.
Over the balcony, once more.

She'd had enough,
she lunged forward,
scratching at my face.

Repelling

I lean back—gradually.

I close my eyes as my heels hang over the edge,
inching farther my shoes curl around the rock.

Beneath my feet, I see the drop. My mouth
rings out a breath to ease the nerves.

With rope in hand
I take the leap,
drifting down,

falling.

With a rush of adrenaline
I squeeze tight my right hand
stopping the fall, my shoes collide
with the wall. I breath out again.

I bend my knees
loosen my right hand
and push off the rock.

In a single leap
I stop just shy
of the ground

I feel
alive.

Near Death

Boots skid over gravel
like roller blades on cement.

A ride not so exhilarating
as my eyes catch wind
of tumbling down.

In an instant a wandering
mind imagines death.

Screams echo—distorted
"Grab Him!"

Gripped from my pack
I'm pulled back as boots
continue to slide.

My ears ring as I
feel the strength.

Breathe in,
Breathe out.

I wonder what
it feels like to fly.

The Best of the Worst Circumstances

"It's like a man's
best party only happens
when he dies." --*Body in a Box* by City and Colour

He searches for the golden gate
as we celebrate life, trapped in a room

filled with more laughter than cries.
A guest list ten miles long, people eagerly

waiting to see the man of the hour. His
suit pressed, his hands locked, eyes shut,

with a smile so inviting; telling the world
to hold on, the party has just begun.

Dreams Come True

You get this idea in your mind
of the way things should be—
wishing to still be dreaming.

Dreams where wishing comes true
and imagination comes alive.

All your thoughts of wants
and desires to go where
bring you the fate you
require.

Take it slow, and ease
into the life you want.

Dreams of the mind are a realization
of things to come. Things that need
to be fought to achieve.

If you think it
you can do it.

If you dream it
make it happen.

You owe it to
yourself
to try.

Secret Family Recipe

The steam rose pulling out
the un-needed liquid and
enhancing the flavor.

Basil fumes in a mesh of garlic,
mint leaves breaking through
the surface, floating idly by
as it steeps
the red.

A spiderweb of spices mixing
with the turn of a wooden spoon.

Watch as they spread
and emerge.

The Expendables

An action packed blur
of explosions booming bright
to mesmerize.

Measuring wits with a smile.
If I had to pick one thing that
I miss, it would have to be this.

All the shitty movies we watched,
the campy action filled seminars
in comfy seats and giant screens.

Big boobs, explosions,
gunfire, and bad-ass lines.

You loved them all, from
raiding tombs to robbing banks,

not to mention fast cars
and police chases.

A man on the run—born against
impossible odds. The lower the
possibility of survival the bigger
the smile.

The bigger the names of the actors,
the harder the pound in your chest.

Well, I'm here to tell you. Dad,
they made a movie with them all.

Hard to Keep Up?

Just you watch me.
I'm capable of so much
more than you think.

I have no limit. Don't listen
to your mom, my knees
will hold up through it all.

I may be old, but I'm still young,
so ask your question again,

I'll keep moving until I die.

A Beautiful Day

It begins and ends with a beautiful day
only now I can see the true beauty:

The tactful necessity of catastrophe,
the sweat tingle on my tongue,
the comfort that I've always needed,
but never thought I wanted.

I wish for the clocks to stay as they are
moving forward at these high speeds.

It's safe to say that I'm happy,

welcoming the creeping tears
knowing I need them, to remind me
of what I had.

I need them
to remind me
of how I got here.

Wilson's Mesa

The huge boulder beneath me, smooth
and crystalline, provides far more comfort

than cushion ever could. Rolling hills off
in the distance. Wind flowing like waves

over mountaintops; a sound you'd have
to hear to believe. Crawling beside me,

a lizard, gravel toned and small, suctioned
to rock, using the shade of my hand; gathered

in refuge in the middle of nowhere, buying
a little rest on the mesa's top.

Questions

It changed me, could you believe it,

not from better to worse
but from worse to better.

I was constantly improving constantly pulling
closer and closer towards the way I should have felt.

But that makes me question,
that makes me wonder. I need
to know:

Who was I?

I was lost and alone,
quiet and confused,
keeping my wits about me.

That was my path.
I didn't need much else,
so I thought.

It makes or breaks you. But why? Why this?

God has a plan I believe or
I WANT to believe

I twiddle, twirl, press, and caress the cross around
my neck with fingertips moist with savory sweat,
through open pours I feel whole again.

Everything happens for a reason
THIS I believe.

But some things just
don't make sense.

Why did this have to happen?

I like to think it took me down
a path of change, towards happiness.

I changed in personality and in thinking,

my thriving heart—mended when I found
the love I was searching for.

I have survived.

My heart told me so,
she told me

I made it out alive.

Part III

Wilson's Mesa. Cimarron, New Mexico. Elevation: 8,619 ft.

With Nothing but a Shadow

After "Mountain Sound," by Of Monster's and Men

following behind as I wallow, drifting
with the horizon pull. Kicks of dirt from

dragging feet polluting the air with a dense
fog. Uneasiness bears upon my shoulders

the weight—wobbling knees; leaving me
unbalanced. With a turn of my head I see,

perched atop skin and bone, the view of the
left behind; a barefoot man calling me home.

An Open Letter

Slowly rotating fan upon a
black end table in the middle
of the room. A twin-sized bed
sheets bundled and used.

An open nightstand drawer:
A box of condoms,
loose change,
a rosary, a lighter,
and a dog tag.

The light above flickers, clashing
against the white paint on the wall.

Hanging nearby a
draping American flag

The stars look like arrows
pointing towards the table below.

On the table it sits, but I can't
bring myself to read it, for fear
of what I might discover.

Snow Shoes and Raw Meet

Heart feels raw within
your chest. In you it feels it

should be cold. You pick at
the seams and peel back

the layers and admire
the craftsmanship of God.

Allude to the thumbs that shaped
and did form the pairing domes.

The clasp that tightened that perfect
pear within your chest. You pick

and observe the flakes that fall
and wonder what makes it beat.

Called back your mother laces your
snow shoes and pins your chest,

sending you away, to gather in swarms
on snow, with the eaters of raw meat.

Threads

Let your hair down slowly
cover and glide, twist and slide
across your face.

I caress as it masquerades
giving a glimpse of mystery.

There you sit, unafraid, holding a
secret behind your curtain threads.

Through the creases I see a
glimmer, the shimmering blue
eyes of a distant stranger waiting
to be released.

Straddled hymn, pulled over, knees
cushioned and bare, entwined,
and eager. While strands cling,

hanging behind while you listen,
thumb over porous cheek, head
brought in with a whisper.

Become Me.

The ringing ears to see
what the eyes did feel
and the heart did flutter.

And curtain strands flipped back
wallowed and relieved with screams.

A pleasure that lay
a sweet flowing lock
upon silk sheets.

Drowning Man

With a click, the easel snaps
into place, unsure it begins
to sink beneath the sand.

The artist holds, observing
the blank slate and breathing in
the scene. His brush, eager

within corroding fingertips
dripping sweat at the sight.
It appears to be a waste,

the paint, a clash upon
the canvas, oozing bright
blue against the backdrop

of the sea. Dazzling sand
bombarding with crisp clean
strokes against a layer

of black. Ease the artist's hand
with a tremor. A shadow,
a distant man yearning

to be seen. His hands toss back,
flailing and screaming. Lost
in the distance but eager

to shine through
the suffocating blue.
The artist sighs and dabs

the brush. Pausing for a moment
as guilt sinks in. He waits.
He thinks. Only to continue.

For this. This
is his masterpiece.
With a flick of the wrist,

he toils the waves. The swoop
the turn, the hand shows
the pull of wind.

Look, feel, and breathe.
The cringe of the water
the grave of a stranger.

Lost at Sea

A tragedy painted with me in mind,
lost in the rising tide, I was pulled

out to sea—tossed about like a rag doll.
Jerking waves crashing endlessly

against the horizon, dragging me
closer and closer to the setting sun.

My body struggled to keep me afloat
as I sank into the bitter cold depths,

drifting downward, the pressure
puncturing my skull, I collided with

the ocean floor. There I sat waiting,
teeth clenched tight refusing to let

go of my breathe. Holding
air in lungs—eager to burst

with spurts breaching the hall,
blue faced cheeks, crackling brain.

The Man in Chains

Awoken within a faceless cave by the torment
of pain and flame—a single lit torch above my

head held to be the only source of light within
this humid corridor. My arms—numb; eyes

fidgeting right then left, I saw that I was chained.
Losing feeling in my legs, I sank, but remained

hanging from the wall. I palmed the moist rock
behind me, listening intently to a constant drip

of water coming from somewhere. I could be
anywhere. I called out for help. My voice echoed

for what seemed like miles. Panic befell on me,
and I began to lose control. The chains shook as I

attempted to rip myself from the wall. I cried in
agony. There was no one, nothing, I was alone.

Empty Shell

"Men go and come, but earth abides."
                --Ecclesiastes, 1, 4.

Lost in an empty world
humanity's slate wiped clean.

Set in the wake of excruciating silence,
wanting desperately for screams
to break through.

Wanting nothing more
than to hear again.

Forced to start over in an empty shell, to abide
in the scintillating glow of the rising sun.
An effervescent shine of hope.

To begin anew.

Grab Hold (With Fear of Falling)

"Wouldn't it be
fine. To stand behind
the words we say." --*Life* by The Avett Brothers

Speak to the fathoms of space
and time— oh! Plummeting waterfall.

Birds above me at a trotter, edging along tight ropes
perched between shoreline and shoreline
feathers dripping—bodies watching.

Under the crosswalk sway, I ride,
tightened rope tied to wooden slabs
hanging on with bobbing words.

From edge to edge crashing rocks
gasping for breath, the water spews
from my pours eager to survive.

Meandering curves—love mending
in hanging arms lush with leaves.

A river crusading—clashing
in bubbling foam.

Pulling river flow
rushing home, crosswinds
and pathways—a snickering phrase.

Distance drops a flock of birds
in a plume of white, passed green
and through green. Leaving behind
that far-flung wall.

Squeamish rapids, rampant
in anguish. Squishing algae
in finger tips—paste to stain.

As I fall behind my words
balance uneasy—dip and cripple.

There I cling, wedged between
rocks teetering edge, as I breath in
the towering splash.

Nose Hairs

Breathe in the sweet
tingling air, the honey

suckle fruit, the albino frost
pulling across the freshly

cut grass. Stuck—so close
you can almost taste it.

All Along

After "Voodoo Child" by Jimi Hendrix

The lighthouse, dull and lifeless, turning light to signal
the sun to set, the beach empty—except for one.

The wind blows the waves into the shore. Tuning in the
pulsating rhythms that flow through my brother's mind.

They ring and slur a slight return. My brother's tiny
fingers—sunburned, dig into a bucket of mud. He pulls,

forms, and shapes a tower in the sand. His left hand edging
close his half sized guitar that never did leave his side.

He dreams big of being a Voodoo Child, the axe is his key,
his ritual. Beside his castle formed a hill of sand that he

chops down with the edge of his hand. A smile burns bright
on his face, the edge of his lips curl as he sees his idol.

Jaw drops in the instant the black soul shoes crunch
against the remains of the hill. *"Hey there Chile."*

the man says, breathing smoke, *"Are you Experienced?"*
Wide mouth, speechless, my brother nods, presenting his

six string soul. Sand dripping from the seams. Jimi
smiles, reaching out the guitar finds its place. He flips

its neck into his right hand. He closes his eyes bringing
a joint to his lips. He inhales and kisses a plume of smoke

into the air; the atmosphere widens and changes. My
brother told me the sky never did looked so blue. All

along the beach Jimi shreds and sings kicking puffs of sand into the air. My brother blinks, shaking his head in disbelief

only to discover, with drooping eyes, that it was too good to be true. He is alone on the beach once more, victim

of his own imagination. Along the pier he hears footsteps staggering by as people flood in. He ignores the noise

and listens to the wind. He can hear her cry, *Jimi*. And he knows, the wind remembers the names it has blown away.

Colors

a heavenly scent of carnations

standing edgeless in waist high
grass, spinning pinwheel child.

Between Two Stone Pillars
After "Marooned" by Pink Floyd

    The vultures circled in a benevolent manor, having the common courtesy to wait till I gave way my final breath. Bright circles crowded my vision. I squinted to regain my sight. Where was I? My entire body was numb, I couldn't move.

    Before me stood, at fifty yards away, a stone pillar that towered over everything, piercing through the middle of the vultures that circled overhead.

    Eyes shifting right, I caught wind of nothing, but to my left, great beauty left me breathless: A cliff that plummeted downward into the greatest sight I have ever beheld; immense waves clashing against the evening shore.

    One tree stood alone in the middle of all the emptiness. The tree was a grand sight; as wide as a church bell and as tall as the stone pillar placed before me.

    My body began to regain its strength, I could move, but as I tried to speak—nothing. The back of my head began to sore, I reached my hand backwards to feel a large rigid object. I curled my head to the side to see what it was I was resting against. It was another stone pillar, in fact larger than the first I had laid eyes on. A curious vulture set foot on the structure, finding it a safe place to wait, it squawked at the others to join him. Some followed and stood beside him, the others remained in place, perched upon the north pillar.

    I felt the coursing wind clash against my face, the breeze filtered through my hair. I breathed in heavily and tried with all my might to stand. Within moments I was at my feet trying to catch my breath. I closed my right eye to block out the bright sun. I glanced to my right once more, I began to feel nervous. Gazing over the horizon as far as my eyes could see, I saw a man, sitting against an old oak tree. He appeared as only a shadow; a faint silhouette of a man. His hands held a book. I could sense that he was looking directly at me, ignoring the book which he held tightly within his palms. He stood up. I felt my heart sink as a tear formed in my eye. I walked towards him, suddenly feeling a snag around my ankle. Looking to see, I realized I was chained. Curious I was more than scared, for it was not the chain of a prisoner, but simply a twine, no smaller than a thread.

I should have felt afraid, but I didn't. I felt some what relaxed. I was in a place unfamiliar to my eyes, but strangely I felt like I belonged. Almost like I had been here before.

Bird calls echoed through the air. I glanced to my left to see a flock of seagulls fluttering over the shore as the waves crashed against the beach. The sounds calmed me. It was like a symphony; the sort of music God would play. And at that moment, I looked to the heavens and raised my hands, trying desperately to scream, but no sound reached my lips.

I felt my face burn red as I tried with all my might; a scream bellowed in my gut. Oh, the power that flung passed vocal cords to enter the sky.

Running with Cheetahs

An embarking journey underneath the boiling desert sun. Hung high the African savanna creeping behind the blackening sky. Heat

streaming from the ground carried upward, piercing the clouds; plucked drain with a whirlpool; a showering rain of sickness.

The growing pit grumbling, harnessed by weak knees wobbling with an unstable pain. The grazing gazelle nervously eating,

swallowing bits of curing grass, boasting in an illusion of false consciousness. Sleeping in the grass in a miserable sulk, hungry

and lonely—in a state of longing the lion dreams his life away, laying in a rising pool, drowning in depression's wake.

Off in the distance, sprinting with leaping bounds, dodging raindrops, pulling away from the storm into the rising sun

the cheetah take his lead into living long. The pain in his hips remain a constant reminder of his survival.

Scattered Stones

Powder snow brushed off boots, lost
above in the heat of the day. Eying the

bundles of trees that surround us; teeming
with green and soulless gallows of trimming

hairs from tree tops fresh with nettles, lush
and gone. Fragments of stones settled beneath

our feet, along the ground from previous
travelers, pointing the way home.

Reminiscing with Dragonflies

After "Dirty Paws," by Of Monsters and Men

Mother nature stands and admires, listening
quietly to the animals speak. Trapped
between cat-tails and blades of grass.

A cricket that creeks, a hopper that weeps, join
in a truthful hymn, swallowed by
the blissful buzz of the bees.

Off sight, hidden within the weeds
a dimming lantern hung high—the post,
slung low, deep into the mucky murk
sinking at the water's edge.

Upon a tarnished bridge
the dragonfly glides and whispers
as mother lets her draped body
hang over the railing edge, fingers
reaching towards the water below

a calloused tear—drip then ripple
a melody streaming with waves that wake
the croaks and the rickets and the fireflies.

Ring with finesse the chanting
ensemble—the frog chorus
and the lady of the forest.

They speak out—against
the clamor of chains,
an outcry of rage,
the engines, and the machines,
and the undertaker.

Upon the Shell of a Turtle

Beneath the wonder that flows, the crystal pure water that
covered the home, a turtle, sturdy and calm

that drifts with the river's pull, slow and unsure
of the world beyond. Unsteady in his gaze he sees

the birds and clings to his shell, nervous, trapped
he feels and dreams of flight through clouds and

sky. Mistaken a bird perches upon his rock-like
shell and sings a melody pure and a melody rare

that rings upon the turtle's back carried out to sea.
A whistle that echoes, bringing in harmonies

colliding against the alabaster cliffs, squeezing
through the forest and clinging to trees,

joining in force with a siren of tweets.
Dusted off wings the bird she flies to join

the branch that sings, leaving behind that lonesome
rock—corroded. Eyes closed he breathes delight

and sinks with the setting sun, as friends did
gather upon his shell.

One White, One Black

with a glide of my hand
and a twiddle of my fingers

sound rise and fall
from treble to bass

melody never seems to find
its place.

beyond middle C,
a step:

One White
        One Black
One White
        One Black
One White

88 keys
a chromatic crawl
rising to the top

with a minor crash
melody is lost

the saving grace
a step:

        One White
One Black
        One White
One Black
        One White

fall back
to C

Balloon

Held down by a string
like gallant propaganda
my heart, a lion

full to burst, swinging
eyes look up into the sky;
unstoppable me.

Above I disappear, leaving
the others to wonder
if I'll ever return.

The Necklace (A Climb Back Up Part 2)

Your voice hits me with a chilling calm,
and smiles at my accomplishments. With

so much admiration I feel uneasy. I look to
you to believe, but it can't be true. Can it?

You stand before me, right hand on my
shoulder telling me everything will be just

fine. You tell me you're gone and that
this will be our final meeting.

Around my neck you place a little piece
of you, something to remind me that you will

always be with me. You turn me 'round and send
me packing, telling me, "*Move fast. A storm is*

coming." My head doesn't want to listen, but my
feet oblige. I begin my descent. As I pull down

the mountain, the clouds begin to pour, I let myself
soak. As my boots shift along the path, the ground

begins to dampen as water seems to rise from
the earth. The trail turns into a river, the water

seeping through my wool socks—drenched, I begin to
lose feeling in my arms and legs. The raindrops seize

as hail takes their place. The drops bruise me, but
I carry on. There will be warmth at the end of the

trail, I can feel it. At the bottom I take shelter in a
shack. I feel the man around my neck while I

struggle to breathe. My lips—purple, my body,
trembling, so uncomfortably I can hear my bones

rattle. I feel they will shatter. I rub my
shoulders trying to bring life back to my core.

I feel the man running within my chest. My heart
ignites a bursting flame. In an instant the rushing air

returns to my lungs, my skin begins to smooth, and my
lips shade to pink. I gaze into the sky mesmerized,

the sun peaking through the blackest cloud. I
pull myself to my feet. And as I feel the ground

lifting me up, I can see what I need. I find the
words around my neck and bring myself to climb

again. Through the rushing water and falling rocks,
the trees palpitating ice as I move; held back by

nothing. As I breach the summit I look around to
find myself alone.

He truly is gone.

But I don't cry. I don't wince. I don't fall to my knees. I
gaze over the edge letting my feet hang over, wobbling

letting the wind make its choice. But I know I won't
fall. My neck burns bright red as it builds to scream;

the words hit the roof of my mouth chill and calm.
"ANOTHER BEAUTIFUL DAY!"

This is me.
I made it out alive.

Thank you for taking this journey with me. This is the view from the top.

Acknowledgments:

The Avett Brothers. *The Carpenter*. Universal Republic, 2012. CD.

City and Colour. *Bring Me Your Love*. Vagrant Records, 2008. CD.

Jimi Hendrix. *Expierence Hendrix: The Best of Jimi Hendrix*. Sony Music Australia 1997. CD.

Of Monsters and Men. *My Head Is an Animal*. Universal Republic, 2012.

About the author:

Matthew Cipolla is the youngest of five from Canton, Michigan. He is currently a student at Central Michigan University working towards a major in English with a Creative Writing concentration as well as a major in Anthropology, with a minor in Sociology. He intends to graduate in December, 2013. Matt is a poet, author, and musician. He believes that the key to being a successful writer is finding inspiration. His inspiration comes from three simple words spoken by his father Frank Cipolla: "Another beautiful day." This is the idea that everyday is beautiful, no matter what the circumstance; rain or shine, beauty is everywhere.

Notes:

www.ingramcontent.com/pod-product-compliance
Lightning Source LLC
Chambersburg PA
CBHW051707040426
42446CB00008B/758